The Camper Van Coloring Book

The Camper Van Coloring Book

SIRIUS

SIRIUS

This edition published in 2024 by Sirius Publishing, a division of
Arcturus Publishing Limited,
26/27 Bickels Yard, 151–153 Bermondsey Street,
London SE1 3HA

ISBN: 978-1-3988-4331-8
CH012203NT

Printed in China

Introduction

Do you dream of a life—or just a holiday—out on the open road? In a camper van, ideally a characterful vintage VW version? Feed the dream with this coloring book packed with fantasy vans with their own unique decorations. There are flowery vans, peace vans, surf vans, and many incarnations in between, all channeling the free spirit that these iconic travel wagons evoke. In between the vans, there are images of places you might see on your travels, including Paris and Pisa, country paths and forest walks, picnicking places, and campsites. All are designed to inspire both those who actually travel and the armchair dreamers. All you need is a set of colored pens or pencils, a place to work, and your imagination!

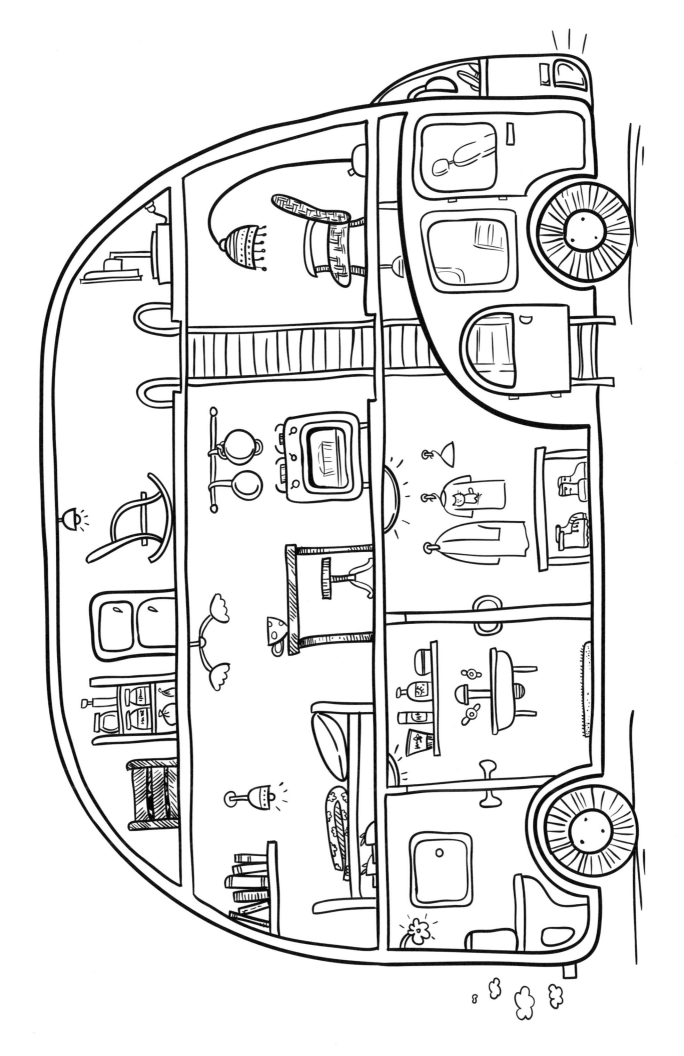

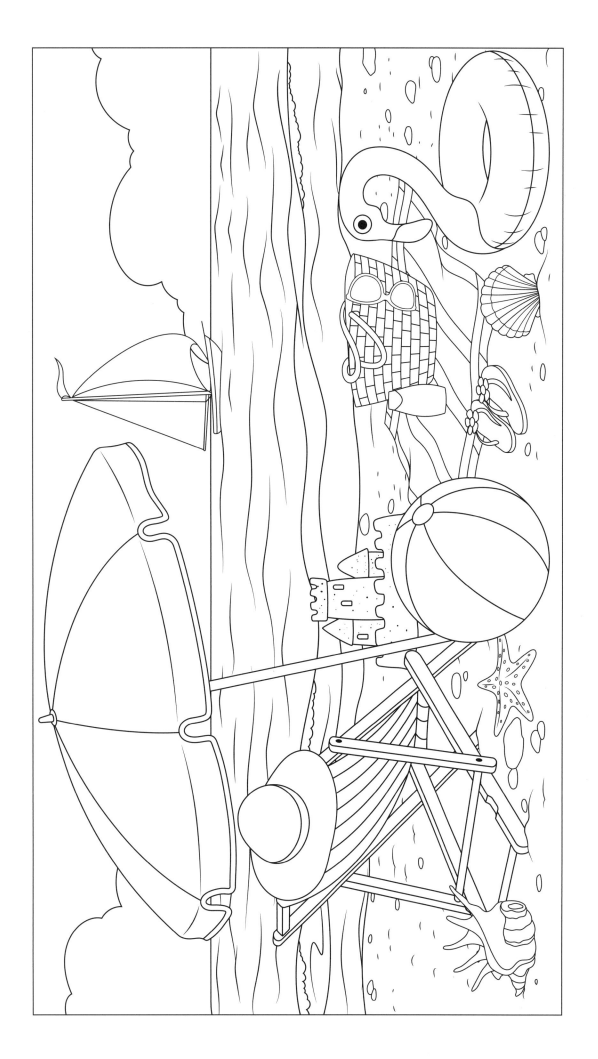

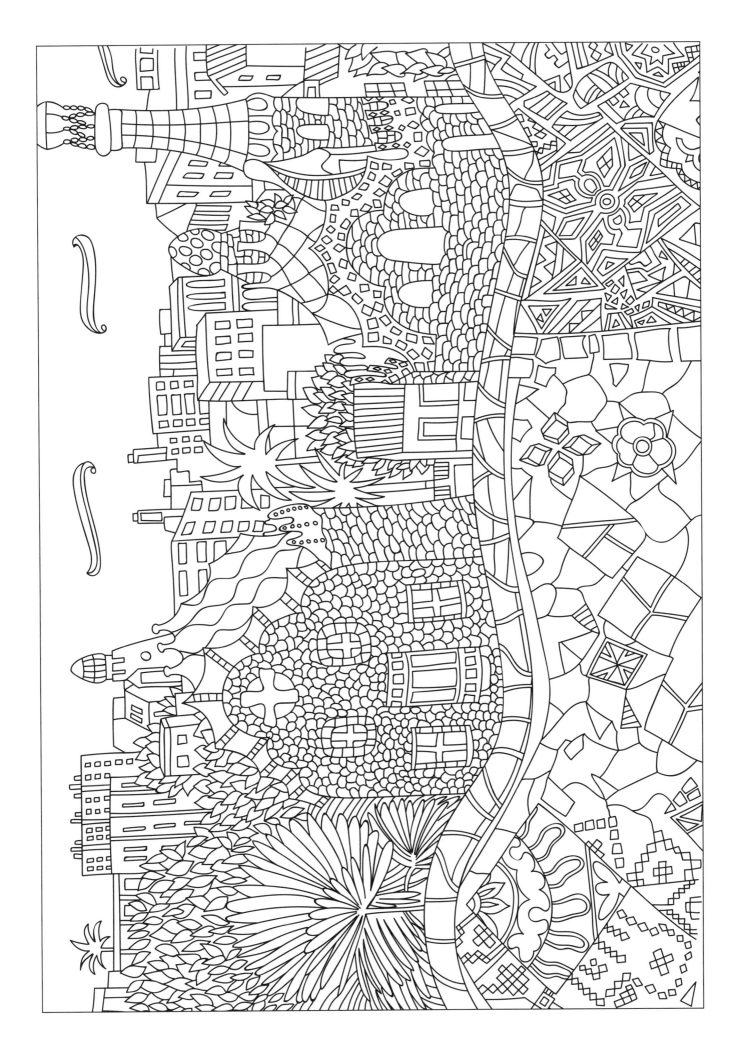

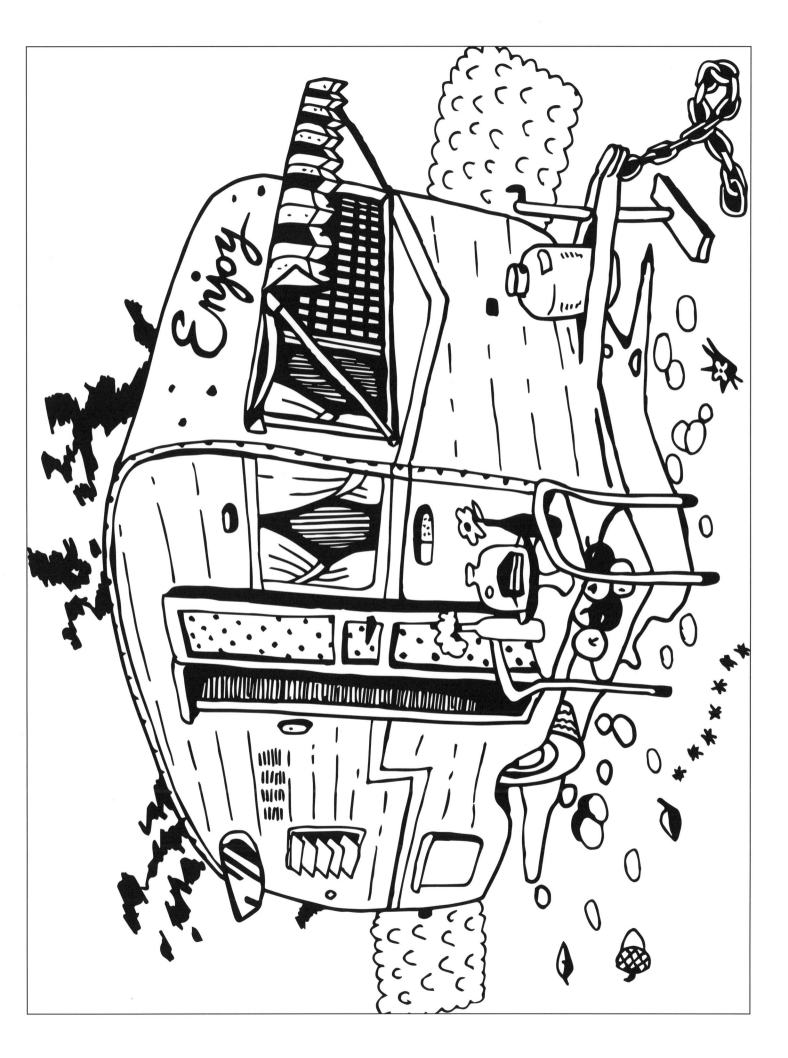

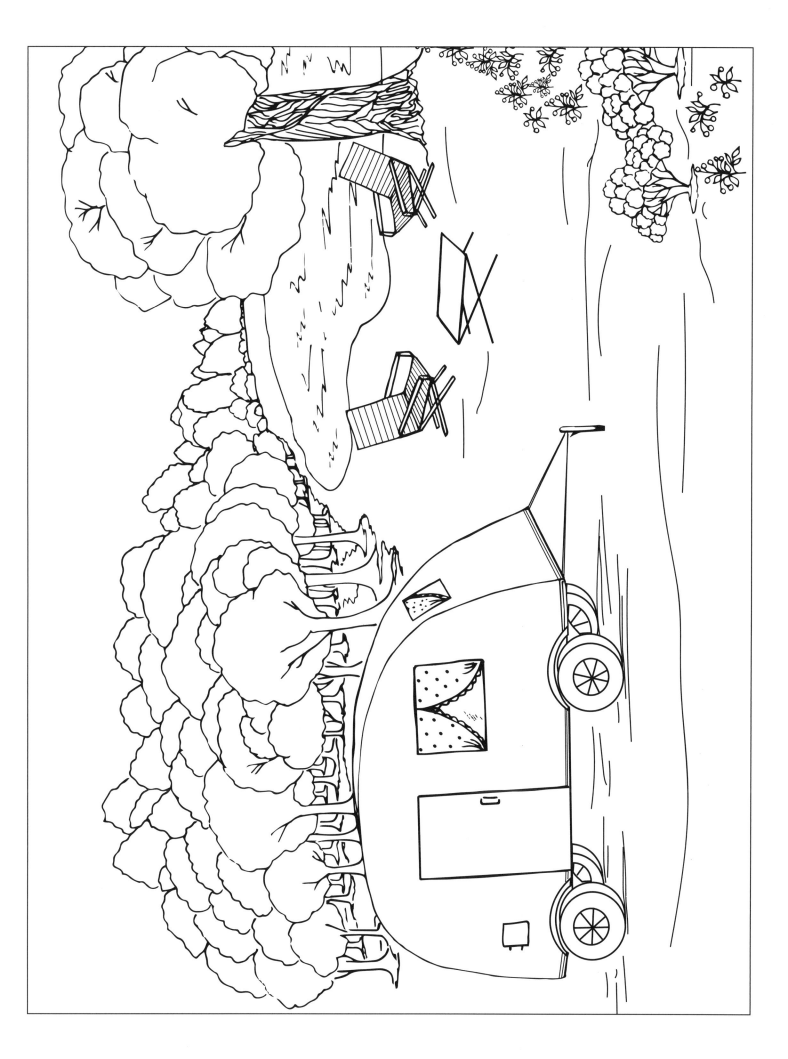

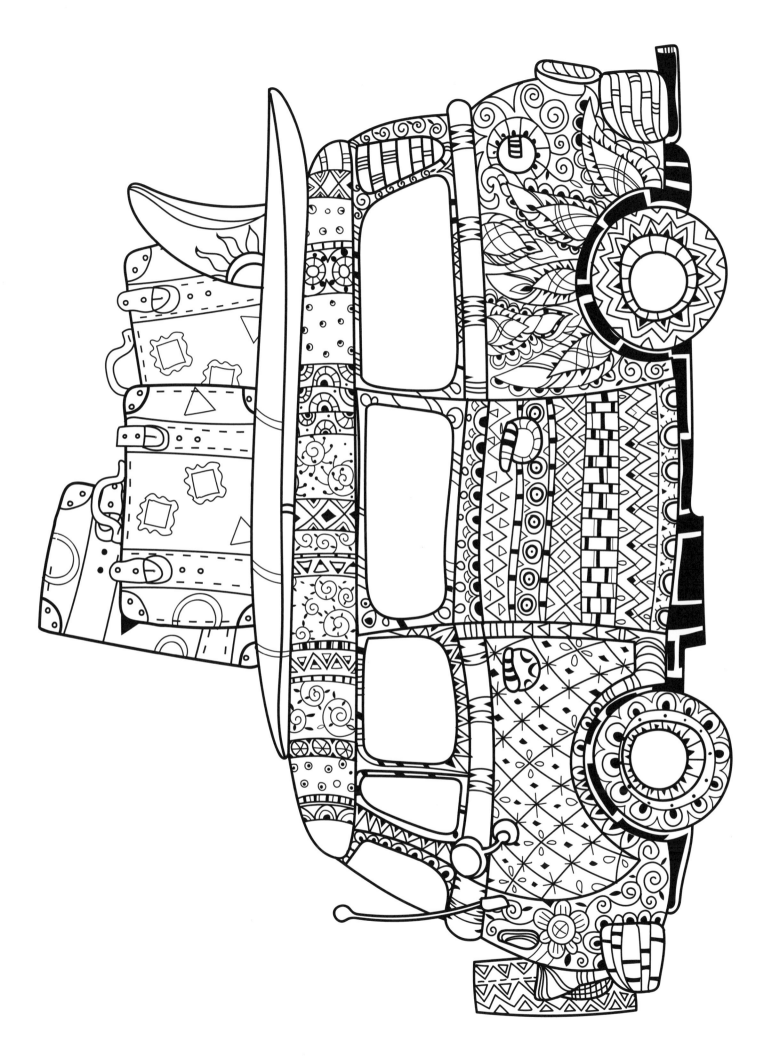

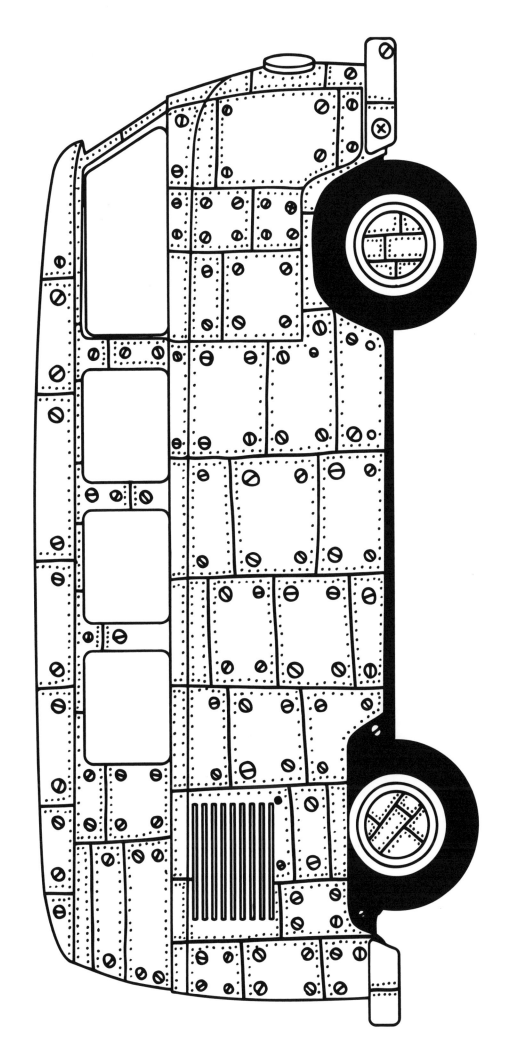

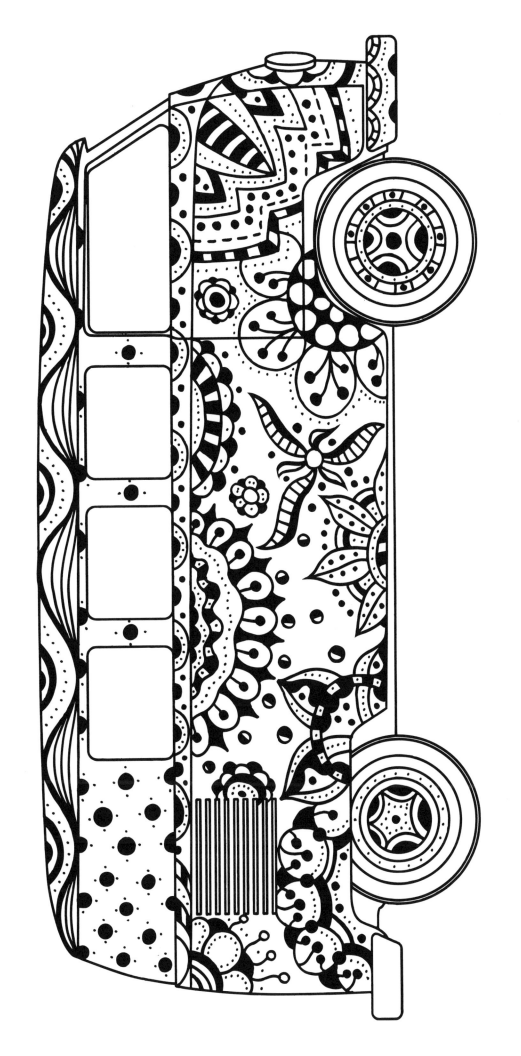

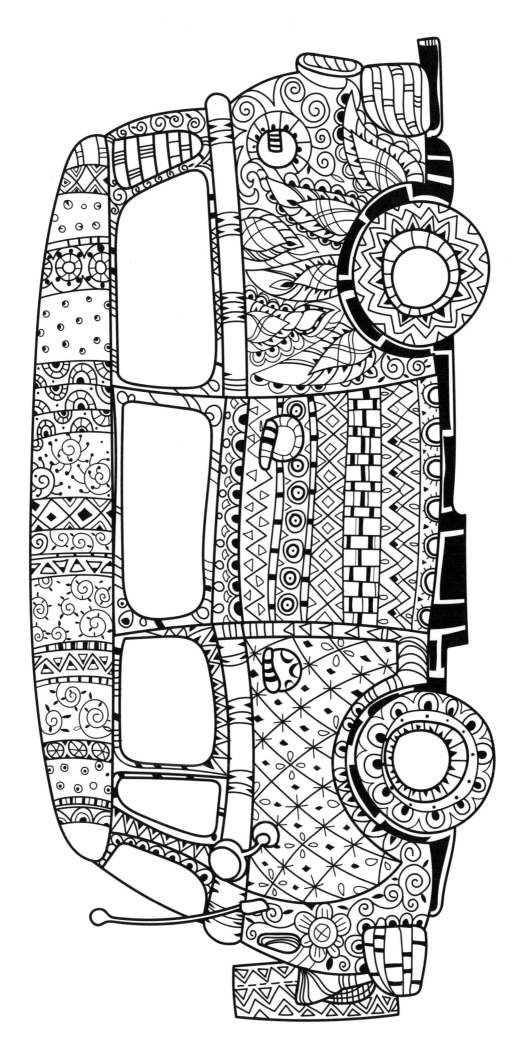